The Palette of Words

Poems

by

Yuu Ikeda

Lighted Lake Press

The Palette of Words: Poems

ISBN-13: 978-0-9969627-2-8

Library of Congress Control Number:
2022905599

Lighted Lake Press
Topeka, Kansas

Acknowledgments

I would like to thank these journals for publishing my poems:

Discretionary Love (*Untitled*),
GLITCHWORDS (*Loneliness*),
Lothlorien Poetry Journal (*Courage*),
Overachiever Magazine (*VACUITY*),
Poetry and Covid (*Dawn*),
Re-Side (*Warning*),
Seedling Poets (*Always*),
ShabdAaweg Review (*Perpetuity/Rust*)
talking about strawberries (*Rain*),
Tealight Press (*Seeds*),
Whispers and Echoes (*Growth*).

Afterglow.................................3

Always.................................4

Ambivalence.................................5

Automatically.................................6

Ballad.................................7

Blue.................................8

Constellation.................................9

Courage.................................10

Dawn.................................11

Destiny.................................12

Dewdrops.................................13

Evidence.................................14

Eyelids.................................15

Flame.................................16

Glimmer.................................17

Growth................................18

Hallucination................................19

Happiness................................ 20

Hope................................21

Inversion................................ 22

Jigsaw................................ 23

Kindle................................ 24

Lamentation................................25

Loneliness................................ 26

Melody................................27

Moonlight................................ 28

Moonrise................................ 29

Never................................30

Nightfall................................31

Nightmare................................ 32

Overdose..33

Overture..34

Perpetuity...35

Poetry..36

Quiver..37

Rain...38

Repentance...39

Runaway...40

Rust..41

Sanctuary...42

Seeds...43

Sorrow...44

Temporary..45

Tragedy..46

Undulation..47

Untitled...48

VACUITY..49

Vow...50

Warning..51

Woe...52

X-ray...53

Yawn...54

Zero...55

About the Author.................................57

A1

Afterglow

Afterglow is fragments of you.
It always sinks to the bottom of the world,
but always remains in the bottom of me.
I can hear blood-red screams.
I can see the bloodless face.
I can love the dull eyes
eternally.

A2

Always

Fragments of your heartbeats
are the necklace
that I wear.

Always,
I feel that
you breathe
on me.

Fragments of your heartbeats
are the ring
that I wear.

Always,
I feel that
you sigh with relief
on me.

Mixture of desire and healing
cocoons you and me.

A3

Ambivalence

Ambivalence that holds its breath in me
reflects off the horizon that soaked in dusk.
An ugly bluff crumbles in me,
and spreads every inch of my veins.
Cursed tomorrow waits for me
to decide the end or the beginning.
I can't escape from the decision.
I must not be cocooned
in thirst for sleep,
until the decision stupefies my night.

A4

Automatically

I'm automatically
lured into the rising sun.
Although I'm a child of night,
I'm in love with the light like a ruby.
In my blood,
profuse fragments of orange
are sleeping.
I feel them, always.
I crave them, always.

B1

Ballad

With winter wind,
the holy ballad flows
into my room
from the broken window.
As if time gave up going to the future,
the holy ballad stops everything
that my brain feels.
I'm cocooned in the sound of vacuity.
Nothing is here.
Only me.
Only the holy ballad.

B2

Blue

Your eyes are covered with blue.
The blue is passion.
The blue is fire.
The blue is depression.
The blue is disappointment.
The blue is hope.
The blue is lamentation.
Your blue changes into
a variety of blue.
Your blue dyes yourself
waves of blue.
I always see colorful blue in your eyes,
these blue burn in your eyes,
and these blue let a lot of flowers bloom
in your eyes.

C1

Constellation

If you become a constellation,
I also become a constellation.
If you choose to live on the sky forever,
I don't hesitate to live on the sky forever.
If you dust brightness on this world,
I also dust the brightness on this world.
If you are tired from shining,
I become a blanket of darkness.

C2

Courage

Fear is a crack of courage.

From the crack,
tears drop
like moonlight does,
waves of tremble resound
like a symphony does.

But
courage never breaks.

Courage
that braced to feel fear
never breaks
even if invisible fear
makes it bloody.

Courage has a crack.

Into the crack,
waves of strong breath flow
like sunlight does.

D1

Dawn

My brain draws
dawn that I saw with you.
The dawn was hope
that I could run toward
new colors.
The dawn was hope
that I could swim
even in the despairing desert.

D2

Destiny

Destiny is like the blue sky
that I look up when I'm in love.
It never changes.
It is always clear blue.
Destiny is like the gray sky
that I look up when I'm in broken heart.
It never changes.
It is always deep gray.

D3

Dewdrops

They fascinate me stronger
than a diamond does.
On picturesque leaves,
they are waiting to vanish.
Like night becomes smoke
and disappears from the stage,
they vanish from leaves.
I don't touch them.
Instead of it,
I write them
to carve them on my notebook.

E1

Evidence

Kiss my shadow of sadness,
and dye it your despair.
If your despair is stronger
than my sadness,
I can forget myself and
can feel yourself together.
Even if a piece of the despair
sinks to the bottom of me
and fills there with needles,
I want to feel what you feel,
because
being your tranquilizer
is the only evidence
that I am alive.

E2

Eyelids

Your eyelids are dyed in relief.
I kiss your eyelids,
not lips,
not cheeks.
Your eyelids are the evidence
that you love me and I love you.
You hide burning blue
behind eyelids.
So, I kiss your eyelids.

F

Flame

Flame of madness
is blinking at the depths of me.
The heat makes me blind.
The intensity makes me silent.
Dancing to an unknown waltz,
flame of madness
circulates through my body...

G1

Glimmer

A glimmer like the sound of the harp
flickers around me.
Between despair and resignation,
the glimmer emits a faint hope,
and casts a shadow of prayer.
I'm feeling it now,
between despair and expectations.

G2

Growth

floating rising sun
misty sky spreading the veil
a mixture grows in a glow

H1

Hallucination

I'm in hallucination
that death opens its bloodless eyes
and smiles at me.
The dreamlike warmth
is waiting for me
on my bed.
Every morning,
I'm drunk on the shadow of death.

H2

Happiness

Happiness covers my eyes
with misty smoke,
and
overclouds my hands
that try to write loneliness.
Happiness fills my ears
with mellow sounds,
and
overclouds my hands
that try to give me
pain caused by loneliness.
Happiness makes
my notebook blank.
Although my pen runs around pages,
happiness becomes a high wall
between the ink and pages.

H3

Hope

I feel the transient hope
crouching in lamentation.
I feel the fragile hope
looking up at the sky
at the bottom of thick despair.
The hope like a light snow
reflects drops of lamentation,
and looks bright.
The hope like spring haze
swallows smoke of thick despair,
and is eddying deeply and mysteriously.
Someday,
the hope like a light snow
will become a streak of vehement fire
that burns pains
and heals my broken heart.
Someday,
the hope like spring haze
will become a fragment of light
that eases darkness
and warms tears calmly.

I

Inversion

It is so difficult
to understand Human beings.

They express love
as if it is reflected in a mirror

ΓΟ∧Ε

J

Jigsaw

The theory of love
is like a jigsaw puzzle.
I don't have enough brain
to solve the puzzle.
On a palm of love,
I'm just wandering
with fears of its vulnerability.

K

Kindle

Night wind kindles my desire
to be cocooned in
a shroud of eternal darkness.
There is no one.
There is nothing.
Only me and relief.
Only warmth and me.
Infinite serenity welcomes me.

L1

Lamentation

Every night,
the moon laments me,
and drops tears
on my notebook.
These marks become vague silhouettes,
and fill it with unlimited words.
I don't cry,
because the moon is crying
only for me.

L2

Loneliness

Loneliness is fireworks.

It changes colors and shapes,
and dyes night itself,
dyes my heart itself.

Loneliness is fireworks.

It vanishes every morning,
to be mystery.
But it appears every night,
to be flowers.

M1

Melody

Melody is running,
not in my room,
but on my notebook.
Tones of my sigh
are the symbol
that life goes on.
Even in the darkest era,
I can make melody run
on my notebook.

M2

Moonlight

The sound of love
is like Debussy's Moonlight.
Ripples of heartbeats
count days when I'm with you.
Raindrops vanish,
the sun always laughs,
and wind whispers to me,
"What you are feeling now
is called First Love."

M3

Moonrise

I'm listening to your whisper and breath.
The dull sun shrinks back
from the world,
the horizon allows night to spread,
then,
the moon blooms in the sky.
I'm listening to your whisper and breath.
The fragile and bright silhouette
is like silent healing music.

N1

Never

I have the background
like the evening glow.
You have the background
like the morning glow.
So, we are never able to thaw together.
We are never able to mix together.
When I sink to darkness
full of emptiness,
you are afloat on brightness
full of petals of hopes.
When I'm a moon,
you are a sun.
When I'm night,
you are morning.

N2

Nightfall

In a cocoon of nightfall,
a firefly is floating,
as if an invisible fairy
writes letters on the canvas of darkness.
I trace the road of a faint light
to feel sorrow that dawn surely comes.
I gaze at the vulnerability
not to forget the joy that
night comes again.

N3

Nightmare

As if I took a roller coaster,
I dive into a nightmare.
My heart beats fast,
my brain wanders slowly.
Waves of change
take my reason away,
and give me silent tears.
This nightmare
never lets me go.
It is just creeping
on me
like an insect does.
As if I took a roller coaster,
I'm pulled by a nightmare.
My heart is about to stop,
my brain is about to thaw.
Where is my reason...?

O1

Overdose

I overdose on inks of tones
but I can't make any melodies.
I overdose on inks of letters
and,
I can fill my notebook
with melodious
(sometimes cracked) poems.
I'm a genius in overdose.

O2

Overture

Vanity is the overture of torment.
An Ego is the overture of destruction.
I'm in both of the overtures.

P1

Perpetuity

A glass of brandy
tries to lure me.
When I drink it like Ambrosia,
I may be able to write death.
When I understand perpetuity,
I may be able to understand death.

P2

Poetry

Poetry helps me breathe.
Poetry allows me to breathe.
Always,
I'm alive with poetry.
Poetry helps me swim.
Poetry allows me to swim
in this world full of words.
Always,
I'm alive with poetry.

Q

Quiver

Quivering fingers
touch my left earring.
The color is sapphire.
My left ear flushes,
your fingers are clothed in heat.
A gleaming candle in gloom
celebrates this momentary night.
A tattoo of a butterfly on your neck
soars in this vulnerable night.

R1

Rain

Rain is crying
behind the sun.

I'm feeling you.
I'm breathing in your scent.

Rain is wailing
behind the sky.

I feel like touching your pain.
I feel like shouting my pain.

R2

Repentance

I inhale guilt,
and exhale guilt.
I have no way
to repent.
Every day,
guilt piles up
in my blood
little by little.
Someday,
this shapeless guilt
will cover my veins
and
stop a blood current
to my heart.
When this heart stops,
repentance is realized.
Sole light of repentance
brightens the end of my life.
Ugly and dirty soul
is released from guilt.

R3

Runaway

She is running away
from a mouth of pressure
that tries to swallow her gleaming world.
She is running away,
to protect her echoing world
where she can plant
seeds of hopes again and again.
Runaway is her sole shield.
Runaway is her sole bravery.
Runaway is her sole sun.

R4

Rust

Rusty life ties me
to this discolored world.
The fuse to death is ready
to rampage in me,
but the scent of rust
keeps me from beginning to run.

S1

Sanctuary

Here is a sanctuary.
Nobody can dominate.
Whirling emotions
are the evidence that
I have a sanctuary.
The more thorns I feel,
the more emotions rampage here.
The more affection I feel,
the more emotions float here.

S2

Seeds

Seeds that I planted
are remainders of my rotten past.

Muddy present
waters these seeds
and
they grow uglily
like my heart does.

Bloody future
gives them sunlight
and
they grow emptily
like my heart does.

S3

Sorrow

Spring has sorrow.
The sorrow echoes.
The echo dyes
the morning glow pastel orange.
I have sorrow.
The sorrow waves.
The waves dye
the evening glow pastel pink.
Our sorrow is
a part of colors of this world.
Our sorrow moisturizes
this ground and us.
Raindrops of sorrow
become tears of hopes
to feel the new beginning.

T1

Temporary

Happiness made by hidden truth
is a temporary drug
that circulates in our fake souls.
We want the vulnerable
and ugly drug,
whenever we feel disappointment
at this world.

T2

Tragedy

She is standing
at the center of tragedy
made by herself.
She is a master of tragedy.
She is a main cast
of tragedy.
A profusion of
cheering and applause
showers her,
and
she can be cocooned
in cruel calmness.
Although she is standing
at the center of tragedy,
she feels burning satisfaction.
To feel it,
she continues to make
a variety of tragedy.

U1

Undulation

You always ignite
my undulation of love.
Can you hear my heartbeats
that crave you desperately?
Can you see my eyes
that try to tell you that
I love you overwhelmingly?

U2

Untitled

As if the moon is
merry on night,
I'm in love with you.

You spread a blanket of darkness,
and I blink on the silk.

Even when
shining stars don't exist,
I can see you
through my light.

V1

VACUITY

She clings to
a string of vacuity
to float on her life.

Balloons full of vacuity
decorate her life.
She always looks at them,
holding a string of vacuity.

Vacuity becomes a shield
to protect her from every pain.
Vacuity becomes a match
to dissolve her every pain.

So, she clings to
a string of vacuity.

V2

Vow

The holy vow is falling,
on the ground of the holy day.
An angel's breath
changes into snowflakes,
and piles up
as fragments of celebration.
Resounding happiness
mixes with sigh of love,
and wraps us
in perfumed magic.

W1

Warning

A yellow light
of warning
rampages through
my blood vessels,
to tell me that
the bomb of
disappointment
is about to explode
in me.

I know it,
I feel it,
and I hope it,
because
the moment of explosion
is the end of torture.

W2

Woe

The blood-red sunset
dyes the horizon my woe.
On my cheeks,
on my lips,
the color spreads.
I open the window
to feel the red.
I open my eyes,
lest I forget the red.

X

X-ray

Dear Doctors.
My bones are crumbled
by the weight of disappointment.
A bandage is useless to my bones,
because only expectations
are the sole remedy to cure them.

Y

Yawn

When stars yawn,
every light stops shining.
I love them who are bored
with illuminating the world.
When stars yawn,
I breathe a sigh of joy.
I'm waiting that
stars sleep
and the moon gives upon them.

Z

Zero

The number of my life is Zero.
Shapeless, hopeless,
useless, sapless,
faceless, bloodless...
I call it Zero.
No startline.
No goal.
Only Zero.

About the Author

Yuu Ikeda is a Japan based poet. She loves
writing, drawing, and reading mystery novels.
Her poems can be found in *Nymphs, Selcouth
Station Press, Sublunary Review, Remington
Review, Sad Girl Review*, and more. She also
writes poetry on her website:
https://poetryandcoffeedays.wordpress.com.
Her previous poetry collection is *Living in
Nightmares with Few Dreams*, published
under the pen name D. Rose. She posts on
both Twitter and Instagram under
@yuunnnn77.

Made in the USA
Coppell, TX
11 September 2023

21471151R00039